HOW TO ATTRACT WHAT YOU WANT

THE VIBRATIONAL POWER OF PRAYER

GODWIN DARAMOLA

HOW TO ATTRACT WHAT YOU WANT

THE VIBRATIONAL POWER OF PRAYER

GODWIN DARAMOLA

PREFACE

In a world filled with uncertainty and chaos, prayer remains a powerful tool for connecting with something greater than ourselves. Yet, many of us struggle to make our prayers effective, wondering if our words are being heard or if we're simply speaking into the void.

What if you could tap into the vibrational power of prayer to manifest your deepest desires and transform your life? What if you could harness the energy of your thoughts and intentions to bring about real change?

This book reveals the secrets to unlocking the full potential of prayer, showing you how to align your thoughts, emotions, and beliefs to attract what you want. Through a combination of spiritual principles, scientific insights, and practical exercises, you'll discover how to:

- Tap into the vibrational frequency of your desires
- Let go of limiting beliefs and negative patterns
- Focus your intentions with clarity and purpose
- Trust in the universe's plan and timing

Get ready to experience the transformative power of prayer like never before. May this book guide you on a journey of deeper connection, inner peace, and the manifestation of your dreams.

ACKNOWLEDGEMENT

As I reflect on the journey that has brought this book to life, I am filled with gratitude for the countless individuals who have supported and guided me along the way.

To the countless individuals who have shared their stories of transformation and healing through prayer - your testimonies have been a beacon of hope and a reminder of the power of faith.

To my editor, Tawo Kathleen Chidinma, whose skillful guidance and expertise have helped shape this book into its final form - your dedication and passion for excellence are deeply appreciated.

To my graphics designer, Chidiebere Grace, whose creative vision and talent have brought the essence of this book to life - your contribution is a beautiful reflection of the vibrational power of prayer.

To the universe, for the natural guidance and vibrational resonance that have flowed through every word and page - may this book be a reflection of your love and wisdom.

And finally, to you, the reader, for entrusting me with your time and attention - may this book be a source of inspiration, comfort, and transformation in your life.

May our collective vibrational frequency be elevated by the power of prayer, and may love, light, and wisdom guide us all.

With deepest gratitude and appreciation,
Godwin Daramola.

CONTENTS

ACKNOWLEDGMENT	2
PART ONE: INTRODUCTION	8
My Spiritual Journey	9
PART TWO: PRAYER	13
Origin Of Prayer	14
The Importance Of Prayer	20
Types Of Prayers	22
Prayer Posture	32
PART THREE: PRAYER ACCORDING TO ME	34
My Definition Of Prayer	35
Who Answers Prayers?	39
PART FOUR: SECRETS OF THE UNIVERSE	42
Energy	43
Spirituality	44
Law Of Attraction	47

CONTENTS

The Power Of Vibration	50
The Universe And Nature: Systems, Not Creators	52
Religion	55
PART FIVE: PRAYING WITH ENERGY	64
Vibrational Power Of Prayer	65
How To Activate The Vibrational Power Of Prayer	67
PART SIX: LIGHT LANGUAGE	80
THE LANGUAGE OF ENERGY: Unlocking the Power of Light Language	81
PART SEVEN: UNDERSTANDING PRAYER BLOCKAGES	88
The Impact Of Negative Energy And Timing	89
Negative Energy - The Unseen Barrier	89
Timing: The Nature Schedule	93

CONTENTS

PART EIGHT: GRATITUDE	98
Gratitude: Prayer With Vibrational Power	99
CONCLUSION	114
Q & A SECTION	116

PART ONE: INTRODUCTION

MY SPIRITUAL JOURNEY

'You create your thoughts, your thoughts create your intentions; and your intentions create your reality.'
WAYNE W. DYER
(Everyday Wisdom For Success)

As I reflect on my spiritual journey, I am reminded of the profound impact that prayer has had on my life. Growing up in a Christian household, I was taught the importance of prayer from a young age. My family's daily devotions, grace before meals, and active participation in church activities instilled in me a deep appreciation for the power of prayer.

However, as I matured in my spiritual journey, I began to realise that prayer was not limited to religious rituals or dogma. I discovered that prayer was a universal language, transcending religious, cultural, and traditional boundaries. Anybody, regardless of background or views, may use it as a powerful instrument.

My curiosity about the nature of prayer led me to undertake extensive fasting and prayer periods. One such experience was a 22-day water fast on a mountain, which I documented on YouTube.[1]

This transformative experience revealed the importance of generating energy frequency for manifestation. I spent hours in prayer, meditation, and contemplation, seeking a deeper understanding of the divine and my purpose.

Through my experiences, I gained profound insights into the essence of prayer, its purpose, and the importance of consistency and dedication. I realised that prayer was not just a means of seeking answers but also a powerful tool for manifesting our desires.

I learnt to harness the energy of prayer to bring about tangible changes in my life and the lives of those around me.

As I continued on my spiritual journey, I completed a 70-day marathon fast as well as a month-long 6 a.m.–6 p.m. fast, among other spiritual disciplines. Each experience deepened my understanding of the dynamics of prayer and the importance of cultivating a deep, personal relationship with the divine.

I gained an understanding that prayer was a universal language that anybody could learn and that it was not constrained by barriers related to religion, culture, or tradition. I learnt to approach prayer with an open heart and mind, without judgement or expectation.

In this book, I invite you to join me on a journey to explore the spiritual science of prayer. Together, we'll delve into the dynamics of effective prayer. I'll share practical principles and techniques to help you cultivate a deep, personal relationship with nature.

We'll explore the importance of generating energy frequency for manifestation, how to harness the power of prayer to bring about tangible changes in your life, and how to overcome obstacles and challenges through prayer.

My hope is that this book will inspire you to deepen your

understanding, practice of prayer, and discover the secrets to manifesting your desires with clarity and purpose.

Welcome to a spiritual exploration that will revolutionise your prayer life and yield tangible, undeniable results.

Join me on this journey as we unlock the full potential of prayer and discover the transformative power of this universal language. Let us embrace the spiritual science of prayer and manifest our dreams and desires with clarity and purpose.

PART TWO: PRAYER

ORIGIN OF PRAYER

'I have been driven many times upon my knees by the overwhelming conviction that I had no where else to go. My own wisdom, and that of all about me, seemed insufficient for the day.'
~ABRAHAM LINCOLN~

Prayer is a concept that is well known across all spiritual, religious, and cultural communities. Each community has their own definitions and meanings to Prayer.

Etymology of Prayer

Prayer is from c. 1300, *preiere*, 'earnest request, entreaty, petition' also 'the practise of praying or of communing with God'. From Old French *prier* 'prayer, petition, request' (12c., Modern French *prière*). From Mediaeval Latin *precaria* 'petition, prayer', noun use of Latin adjective *precaria*, feminine of *precarius* 'obtained by prayer, given as a favour'. From *precari* 'to ask, beg, pray' (from PIE root *prek- 'to ask, entreat').

From mid-14c. as 'devout petition to God or a god or other object of worship' also 'the Lord's Prayer' also 'action or practice of praying'.

Related: *Prayers*. *Prayer-book*, 'book of forms for public or private devotions' is attested from the 1590s. *Prayer-meeting* 'service devoted to prayer, sacred song, and other religious exercises' is from 1780.

Prayer-carpet is by 1861. *Prayer-rug* 'small carpet spread and used by a Muslim when engaged in devotions' is by 1898.

To *not have a prayer,* 'have no chance' is from 1941.[2]

Definition of Prayer

Prayer is a form of religious practice that seeks to activate a volitional connection to some greater power in the universe through deliberate, intentional practice.

Prayer may be either individual or communal and take place in public or in private. It may involve the use of words, a song, or complete silence. When language is used, prayer may take the form of a hymn, an incantation, a formal creedal statement, or a spontaneous utterance by the praying person. There are different forms of prayer, such as petitionary prayer, prayers of supplication, thanksgiving, and worship/praise. Prayer may be directed towards a deity, spirit, deceased person, or lofty idea for the purpose of worshiping, requesting guidance, requesting assistance, confessing sins or expressing one's thoughts and emotions. Thus, people pray for many reasons, such as personal benefit or for the sake of others.

The act of prayer is attested in written sources as early as 5000 years ago. Some anthropologists believe that the earliest intelligent modern humans practised something that we would recognise today as prayer. Prayer is still a very common practice in the modern world.

The English word 'prayer' derives from the Old French *preier* (meaning 'to request'). From classical times, it was used in both religious and secular senses: *precor* include 'to wish well or ill to any one,' 'to hail, salute,' or 'address one with a wish.' The Latin *orare* 'to speak' later took over the role of *precari* to mean 'pray.' Closely related is the Portuguese *perguntar,* 'to ask' and, by extension, 'ask for.' *Pray* is akin to Sanskrit roots, *pracch- prask-, pras* 'interrogation,' and *prcchati* 'he asks'[13]

People see prayer as a way to protect themselves from the unwanted. Due to recent world events, as you can read on *SSPDaily,* many people fear for their lives. Belief in God becomes an ephemeral chance for them to feel protected and safe.

People of all religions, times, and places pray. It shows a lot of faith and can be used to get help, say thank you, or just calm down. No matter what religion or belief system you follow, prayer can look very different. But the point is usually the same: to connect with something bigger than yourself. Let's look at how people of different faiths and beliefs pray and note what is the same and what is different.

Prayer in Christianity

In Christianity, prayer is both a very private act and a public one. Christians think that prayer is a powerful way to talk to God, ask for help, and show appreciation.

The Lord's Prayer
'Our Father, who art in heaven, hallowed be thy name.
Thy kingdom come.
Thy will be done on earth as it is in heaven.
Give us this day our daily bread, and forgive us our trespasses,
as we forgive those who trespass against us,
and lead us not into temptation, but deliver us from evil.
For thine is the kingdom and the power, and the glory,
forever and ever.'

Christ taught his disciples the Lord's Prayer, which is one of the most famous prayers in the Christian faith. It shows how Christians should pray, praising, confessing, giving thanks, and supplicating.

Different Ways to Pray

There are different kinds of prayers that Christians say, such as adoration (praising and honouring God for who He is), confession (begging for forgiveness), thankfulness (expressing gratitude), and supplication (pleading for help). You can say these prayers by yourself or with other people as part of a group worship service.

Islam: A Devotion Based On Rituals

Muslims pray five times every day. Some of the most important things in Islam are called Salah. This is a big part of the faith and way of life for Muslims. It's a prayer that changes the mind, the body, and the spirit.

The Five Prayers in the Morning

Every day, Muslims know exactly when to pray. They should pray five times a day: in the morning, at noon, in the afternoon, at night, and as the sun goes down. Each prayer is unique, with its own words and steps. They do this to show that they love, respect, and follow Allah.

Du'a Means 'Personal Prayer'

Muslims say Du'a, which are personal prayers that can be offered at any time, in addition to the obligatory Salah prayer. Du'a is more flexible because it can be said in any language to ask for help, show thanks, or state personal needs.

Hinduism

With its many gods and customs, Hinduism offers diverse ways to pray. In Hinduism, prayers can vary vastly depending on the area, the community, and the person praying. Also, people worship various animals that personify the deity.

There is even a temple in India that was built just for rats! So, what spiritual meanings_do these animals have for Hindus? Hinduism is very different from Christianity and may surprise those of different faiths.Puja Means Ritual Worship

Some Hindus pray by making offerings to gods, chanting mantras, and doing rituals at home or in shrines. This is called *puja*. It's a way to thank the gods and ask them to help you.

Prayers And Mantras

Mantras are sacred sounds or phrases that Hindus think have spiritual power and say them over and over again. Bhajans, which are devotional songs, are another common way to pray that shows love and respect for God.

Buddhism

Mindfulness and meditation are two of the most important techniques in Buddhism.

Meditation

Buddhism sees meditation as a way to pray because it clears the mind and helps people grow traits like wisdom and compassion. It is a way to get in touch with your true self and the Buddha's guidance.

THE IMPORTANCE OF PRAYER

Prayer is also very important, especially in some traditions.

Prayers for Individuals And Groups

Jewish prayers can be private or for the whole community. People often say their daily prayers alone, ut in synagogues, especially on the Sabbath and during holidays, group prayers are a big part of the service.

Family Ties And a Bond With the Land

Numerous spiritual and alternative viewpoints emphasise the significance of maintaining a connection to family, the natural world, and spirituality. In these locations, prayer is frequently accompanied by rituals, presents, and calls on the deceased.

Prayers for the Earth And Spirit

Folks who live in some places pray to nature—things like the moon, sun, and land—because they think these things are holy. One way to respect these things and ask them to bless you is through dances, songs, and gifts.

Worship of Ancestors

A lot of different cultures respect and ask for help from their dead ancestors through ancestor worship, which includes prayers and gifts. This behaviour shows that people believe there is a connection between the spiritual world and the real world.

Prayer is a way for everyone to show their faith, even though different religions and belief systems use different methods. Talking to God through prayer can help you feel better and figure out what your life's meaning is. You can do this by making time for planned or spontaneous prayers, meditation, or getting together with other people. It's amazing how different faiths are, but also how much we all want to live together in peace and join together. Say that you agree that prayer helps you in some way. Let it bring light and meaning to your life.[4]

TYPES OF PRAYERS

It is challenging to think of the many forms of prayer in terms of strict categorization because they are interconnected and allow for a flow from one to the other. They are enumerated here more on the basis of psychology than on history.

Petition

The role of the request in religion has played such a central part that, by metonymy (using a word for another expected word), it has given its name to prayer.

However contestable this may sometimes be, it is hard to downplay the significance of making a request, be it for achievements, spiritual, or material gifts. The requests that occur most often are for the preservation of or return to sound health, the healing of the sick, long life, material goods, and prosperity/success in one's undertakings.

A request for such goals may be tied to a magical invocation; it may also be a deviation from prayer when it takes the form of a bargain or of a request for payment due: '*In payment of our praise, give to the head of the family who is imploring you glory and riches*' (from the Rigveda the earliest of the sacred scriptures of Hinduism).

Christianity has never condemned material requests but rather has integrated them into a single providential order while at the same time subordinating them to spiritual values. Thus, in essence, though not always in practice, requests are only on the fringe of prayer. As a religion adopts more spiritual goals, the requests become more spiritual. In *Choephori*, a play written by Aeschylus (a Greek tragic poet of the 6th–5th centuries BCE); Electra, the daughter of King Agamemnon, prays, '*Grant that I may be a more temperate and a more pious wife than was my mother.*'

Other examples of the transformation to spiritual goals may be seen in the prayers of the ancient Babylonian and Assyrian kings, who asked for the fear of God rather than material benefits, and that of a priest of the Ewe (a West African people) who even asks of his god, '*That I remain near you and that you remain near me.*'

Confession

The term *confession* expresses, at the same time, an affirmation of faith and a recognition of the state of sin.

In Zoroastrianism, as in ancient Christianity, the confession of faith accompanies the renunciation of demons. *The Confessions of St. Augustine* also illustrates this dual theme.

In a similar fashion, the ancient and primitive recognised that their sins unleash the anger of the gods. To counter the divine wrath, an Ewe, for example, throws a little bundle of twigs—which symbolises the confessor's sins—into the air and says words symbolising the deity's response: 'All your sins are forgiven you.'

The admission of sin cannot be explained only by anguish or by the feeling of guilt; it is also related to what is deepest in humans—i.e., to what constitutes their being and their action (as noted by Karl Jaspers, a 20th-century existentialist philosopher).

The awareness of sin is one of the salient features of religion, as, for example, in Hinduism: '*Varuna* is merciful even to him who has committed sin' (*Rigveda*). Confession is viewed as the first step towards salvation in both

Judaism and Christianity; in Buddhism, monks confess their sins publicly before the Buddha and the sangha (community of monks) two times every month.

Situated at the most personal level, sin places a human being directly before God, who alone is able to grant pardon and salvation. The Miserere (*'Lord, have mercy,'* Psalm 51) of the ancient Israelite king David expresses repentance for sin with an intensity and depth that has a universal value. One of the results of such a dialogue with God is the discovery of the dark depths of sin.

Intercession

Members of primitive societies have a clear sense of their solidarity in the framework of the family, the clan, and the tribe. This solidarity is often expressed in intercessory prayer, in which the needs of others are expressed. In such societies, the head of the family prays for the other members of the family, but his prayers are also extended to the whole tribe, especially to its chief; the primitive may pray even for those who are not members of his tribe (e.g., strangers or Europeans).

Intercessory prayers are also significant in Eastern and ancient religions. In the hymn of the Rigveda, the father implores the god *Agni* (god of fire) for all of those who 'owe him their lives and are his family.' In the Greek play *Alcestis* by Euripides (5th century BCE), the mother, on her death, entrusts the orphans she is about to leave to *Hestia*, the goddess of the home.

Among the Babylonians and the Assyrians, a priesthood was established primarily to say prayers of intercession. Intercession with the divine is aided by an intermediary, such as a minor deity, a human patron (living or dead), a marabout (a temple or mystic believed to have special powers), or a Christian saint, whose mediation ensures that the prayer is effective.

In biblical religion, intercession is spiritualized in light of a consciousness of the messianic mission. Moses views himself as one with his people even when they fail in their duty: 'Pardon your people,' he prays, 'or remove me from the Book of Life.' Such solidarity finds its supreme form in the prayer of Jesus Christ on the cross—'*Father, forgive them, for they know not what they do*'—which St. Stephen (the first recorded Christian martyr) and other martyrs repeated in the course of their sufferings.

Praise and Thanksgiving

Praise in the prayer of primitive people can be traced to

salutations, such as in the prayer of the *Khoekhoe* (of South Africa) to the New Moon— 'Welcome.' Praise among most of the ancient peoples was expressed in the hymn, which was primarily a prayer of praise (whether ritual or personal) for the gift of the created world. Israel praises its Creator for 'his handiwork,' as does the Qurʾān. Contemplation of the majesty of the universe thus often gives rise to a prayer that is not always completely free from pantheism (the divine in all things).

Panthesim can be found all the way from the nature hymns of some East and South Asian religions to the effusions of Jean-Jacques Rousseau, the 18th-century French moralist, embracing the trees and contemplating the sunrise.

Praise—in addition to concerns for the created world—plays an important role in the prayer of mystics, for whom it is a form of adoration. Praise in this instance constitutes an essential element of the mystic experience and celebrates God no longer for his works but for himself, his greatness, and his mystery.

When the great deeds of God are the theme of praise, it becomes benediction and thanksgiving. Even when words denoting thanksgiving are not present, the substance of thanksgiving is manifest—for example, for the Pygmy of Central Africa, who says to his god, '*Waka [meaning God], you gave me this buffalo, this honey, this wine.*' Mealtime prayers, frequently enunciated in both ancient and modern religions, give thanks for the goods of the earth and are linked to the giving of an offering.

In Christianity, Christ is discovered as the gift of God and, in his mission, the economy (or mode of operation) of salvation. Thus, the giving of thanks is viewed as a human response, as a spiritual reaction to the benefit received—i.e., the mediatory work of Christ. Because of the cultivation of this expected response, praise and thanksgiving occupy a central position in Christian prayer and in the liturgy, so much so that its name is given to the Eucharistic Prayer—the Prayer of Thanksgiving.

Adoration

Adoration is generally considered the most noble form

of prayer—a kind of prostration of the whole being before God. Among adherents of indigenous religions, even if the prayer of request is predominant, they are seized with the feeling of fear and trembling before the numen (spiritual power) of all that is *mana* (endowed with the power of the sacred or holy) or taboo (forbidden because of association with the sacred). Names given to the divinity in prayers of adoration express dependency and submission, as, for example, in the prayer of the K'ekchií Indians of Central America: 'O God, you are my lord, you are my mother, you are my father, the lord of the mountains and the valleys.' To express their adoration, people often fall to the ground and prostrate themselves. The feeling of submissive reverence also is expressed by body movements: raising the hands, touching or kissing a sacred object, deep bowing of the body, kneeling with the right hand on the mouth, prostration, or touching the forehead to the ground. The gesture often is accompanied by cries of fear, amazement, or joy; e.g., *has* (Judaism), *hū* (Islam), or *svaha* (Hinduism).

Adoration takes on its fullest meaning in the presence of the transcendental God who reveals himself to human beings in the religions of revelation (Judaism, Christianity, and Islam). In the prophet Isaiah's vision of the holy, which is recounted in the Hebrew Bible (Isaiah 6:3), the seraphim (winged creatures) chant to Yahweh: 'Holy, holy, holy is the Lord of hosts; the whole earth is full of his glory.' This hymn of adoration became a part of the Christian liturgy. The supreme form of adoration, however, is generally considered to be holy silence, which can be found in primitive religion and in ancient religions, as well as in the 'higher' religions, and among mystics, it expresses the most adequate attitude towards the immeasurable mystery of God: 'I am in a dark sanctuary; I pray in silence; O silence full of reverence' (Gerhard Tersteegen, an 18th-century Protestant mystic). Silent adoration is often viewed as the introduction or response to an encounter with the sacred or holy.

Mystical Union or Ecstasy

Ecstasy is literally a departure from, a tearing away from, or a surpassing of human limitations, as well as a meeting with and embracing of the divine. It is a fusion of **being** and **being in** which the mystic experiences a union, characterised as a nuptial union: '*God is in me and I am in him.*' The mystic experiences God in an inexpressible encounter that is beyond mundane human experiences. The mystical union may be a lucid and conscious progression of contemplative prayer, or it may take a more passive form of a '*seizing*' by God of the one who is praying.

The mystic, by his goals and actions, is removed from both the world and himself. He discovers in the light and majesty of the divine his own poverty and nothingness and is thus torn between the contemplation of the greatness of God and his own meagreness. St. Francis of Assisi exemplified this dichotomy in his prayer: '*Who are you, O God of sweetness, and who am I, worm of the earth and your lowly servant?*'

Ecstatic prayer goes beyond the framework of ordinary prayer and becomes an experience in which words fail. Mystics speak in turn of unity (e.g., the 3rd-century-CE Roman philosopher Plotinus), of great pleasure (Augustine), or of intoxication (Philo Judaeus). It is found in the accounts of Hindu, Persian, Hellenistic, and

Christian mystics. '*You are me, supreme divinity; I am you,*' says Nimbaditya. The Sufi (Muslim mystic) Jalāl al-Dīn al-Rūmī sighs in the same words as a Christian mystic, Angela da Foligno: '*I am you and you are me.*' Mechthild von Magdeburg develops the same kind of reciprocity: '*I am in you and you are in me. We cannot be closer. We are two united, poured into a single form by an eternal fusion.*' Such reciprocity, which is so complete that it becomes identity, is the supreme expression of ecstatic prayer. It is found in all of the mystic writings, from the East to the West.[5]

PRAYER POSTURE

As different cultures, religions, and traditions have their own spiritual practices, they also have their own specific postures in which they pray.

Islam

While praying, the Muslim performs a number of movements. This starts with standing. Halfway through the prayer, the Muslim is in a kneeling position; toes, knees, palms, nose, and forehead should touch the ground. At the end of the prayer, the Muslim is in a position where he is on his knees. Exactly how the poses and movements are done differs per denomination.

Judaism

When a Jew prays while standing, he makes a repetitive motion, moving his upper body from front to back. This is not a mandatory move, but it is often done.

Christianity

The posture of a Christian does not matter much, but there are things that you see a lot. For example, when praying, Christians often fold their hands and close their eyes. Some Christians kneel, and others raise their hands.[6] Some Christians bow their heads and fold their hands.

Some **Native Americans** regard dancing as a form of prayer. **Hindus** chant mantras, while some **Sufis** whirl. **Quakers** often keep silent. Some pray according to standardised rituals and liturgies, while others prefer extemporaneous prayers; others combine the two.[7]

PART THREE: PRAYER ACCORDING TO ME

MY DEFINITION OF PRAYER

'I am the master of my fate; I am the captain of my soul.'
WILLIAM ERNEST HENLEY
((Invictus)

As a spiritual leader, I am often asked about my beliefs and practices. Let me be clear: I am not Jesus, nor am I a Christian. My approach to spirituality is rooted in the understanding that prayer is a powerful tool for manifesting our desires.

I conceptualise prayer as a multifaceted spiritual process that facilitates meditation and affirmative declaration. Through this process, individuals can focus their minds and energies on specific desires, thereby manifesting their realisation.

This definition underscores the significance of intentional thinking and visualisation in shaping our experiences and outcomes. By concentrating our thoughts and mental energies, we can tap into the creative potential that underlies all existence, bringing our aspirations into being.

The process of prayer, as I define it, involves a profound

interplay between the individual's inner world and external reality. By aligning our thoughts, emotions, and beliefs with our desired outcomes, we can harness the transformative power of our minds to shape our lives and circumstances.

Prayer, in this sense, is a powerful tool for personal growth and transformation. By focusing our minds and energies on specific goals and desires, we can overcome limitations, challenge negative thought patterns, and cultivate a more empowering mindset.

Moreover, prayer has the potential to foster a deeper sense of connection and oneness with the world around us. By recognising the interconnectedness of all things, we can transcend our individual concerns and tap into a larger sense of purpose and meaning.

Through prayer, we can also access a sense of inner wisdom and guidance. By quieting the mind and listening to our intuition, we can gain valuable insights and perspectives that can inform our decisions and actions.

In addition, prayer can serve as a powerful catalyst for change. By focusing our collective energies and intentions on specific goals and outcomes, we can create a groundswell of support and momentum for positive transformation.

It is important to note that prayer is a highly personal and individualised process. There is no one 'right' way to pray, and individuals can adapt and modify their approach to suit their unique needs and preferences.

Ultimately, my definition of prayer highlights its potential as a potent tool for personal growth, transformation, and manifestation. By harnessing the power of our minds and hearts, we can create a brighter, more fulfilling future for ourselves and those around us.

Prayer is a revered and sacred instrument that enables us to resonate with the fundamental frequency of the universe. This frequency is an invisible yet palpable force that permeates all of existence, originating from the source of all things, the wellspring of life itself.

Through prayer, we can tap into this universal energy, harnessing its power to shape our lives and circumstances. By aligning our thoughts, emotions, and intentions with this natural force, we can manifest our desires and create the outcomes we seek.

In its essence, prayer is a synergy of meditation and affirmation. It involves a deep state of contemplation, where we quiet the mind and focus our attention inwardly while simultaneously affirming our desires and intentions with unwavering conviction.

This sacred practice allows us to transcend our limitations and connect with a higher reality, accessing guidance, wisdom, and inspiration that can inform our decisions and actions. By doing so, we can overcome challenges, overcome obstacles, and achieve our goals.

Prayer has the potential to foster a profound sense of unity and interconnectedness with the world around us. By recognising our intrinsic connection to the universe and its source, we can cultivate empathy, compassion, and understanding, leading to a more harmonious and peaceful existence.

Moreover, prayer has been shown to have a positive impact on our physical and mental well-being, reducing stress, anxiety, and other negative emotions while promoting overall health and resilience.

The power of prayer lies in its ability to rewire our minds with positive thoughts and beliefs, reorienting our perspective and behaviour to align with our highest potential.

By repeating affirmations and visualising our desired outcomes, we can reprogram our subconscious mind and unlock our inner strength and potential.

Furthermore, prayer can serve as a powerful catalyst for personal growth and transformation. By dedicating ourselves to this sacred practice, we can develop greater self-awareness, discipline, and inner peace, leading to a more fulfilling and purpose-driven life.

It is essential to remember that prayer is a highly personal and individualised practice, accommodating diverse beliefs, values, and experiences. There is no one *'right'* way to pray, and individuals can adapt and modify their approach to suit their unique needs and preferences.

Ultimately, prayer offers a profound opportunity to tap into the boundless potential of the universe, harnessing its power to create a life of purpose, meaning, and fulfillment. By embracing this sacred tool, we can transcend our limitations and become the masters of our destiny.

WHO ANSWERS PRAYERS?

The concept of prayer and its associated beliefs have long been a topic of interest and debate. As someone who does not subscribe to any particular religion, culture, or tradition; I have always been skeptical of the idea that prayers are answered by a deity or higher power.

The traditional view of prayer is that it is a means of communicating with a higher power, who then grants answers to our prayers as they see fit. However, I find this perspective to be misleading and lazy. It suggests that we are not responsible for our own lives and that someone else will come to our rescue if we just pray hard enough.

This belief raises several questions. If there is one all-powerful God who answers prayers, why do some people receive answers while others do not? Why can some religious leaders perform miracles through prayer while others cannot, even though they serve the same God? Why do some church members receive miracles and testimonies while others do not, even though they are praying to the same deity?

I firmly believe that there is no deity that answers prayer; rather, we, as humans, are the ones who give answers to our prayers. We are the ones who have the power to create the life we want, to manifest our desires, and to make our dreams a reality. However, we are not willing to put in the work to get the results we want.

Instead of taking responsibility for our own lives, we leave it to our deities or spiritual leaders to do the work for us. We pray for answers, but we do not take the responsibility of being the answer to our prayers. We want someone else to rescue us, to save us, and to fix our problems. But the truth is, there is no god, goddess, deity, or spirit that will come to our rescue. We are the ones who must take the responsibility and duty to be the answer to our prayers.

Later in this book, we will explore the practical steps we can take to manifest our desires and create the life we want. We will learn how to meditate, affirm, raise our frequencies, and cultivate a positive posture to generate the energy required to manifest our desires.

We will learn how to take responsibility for our own lives and be the answer to our own prayers.

PART FOUR: SECRETS OF THE UNIVERSE

ENERGY

'If you want to find the secrets of the universe, think in terms of energy, frequency and vibration.'
NIKOLAS TESLA

Energy is the life force that flows through all things. It is the source of our power and the key to creating anything we desire.

Frequency is the rate at which energy vibrates. This can be measured in hertz (Hz).

Vibration is the amplitude, or intensity, of energy. The higher the vibration, the more powerful the energy.

Everything in the universe is made up of energy, which vibrates at different frequencies. The energy that we emit also vibrates at a certain frequency.

'The universe is energy. Vibrational energy. All energy vibrates. All matter is energy that has slowed down enough so that we can see it and touch it.' —Nikola Tesla

Our thoughts and feelings are energy, and they vibrate at a certain frequency. When we focus our thoughts on something, we emit a signal with a specific frequency. This signal is then broadcast into the universe, and it begins to attract energy that vibrates at the same frequency.

SPIRITUALITY

I see spirituality as a realm of energy. Energy is the language of spirituality. Energy is the source of life. Everything that exists has energy in it.

Energy is the creator of life. Spiritual energy is an invisible force that flows through all living beings, including human beings.

Matter is anything that takes up space and has mass—anything you can perceive in physical form. Think plants, rocks, houses, cell phones, and yes, even you! And science shows energy exists in the building blocks of all matter.

So why does that matter?

Because it means that if everything around you is matter and all matter is energy, then everything is energy!

If you have never been exposed to this idea before, it can be a bit confusing because we are used to thinking about energy from a rational, scientific perspective. You know that energy powers the lights in your house; there are kinetic and potential energies, and energy is behind everything in existence (thanks to Einstein's $e = mc^2$). So what exactly is spiritual energy?

Generally speaking, when you hear spiritual writers talk about energy, they are referring to one of two things.

The first meaning has to do with the universal field of energy, which encompasses everything in existence. If you're religious, you're probably used to hearing about this in terms of God. This field of energy is also accepted by Western science, and, of course, it is well established in Eastern traditions as well. It is the intangible, unknowable field of existence, All That Is, and is also commonly referred to as simply *"The Universe."*

The second meaning is more personal. Many spiritual texts talk about energy in terms of your own individual mindset and state of being. In day-to-day scenarios, you might talk about a person having "high energy" or "low energy" to describe how active they are or how passionate they might be about a project, but in spiritual circles, the meaning is slightly different. Often, high and low energy refer to a person's mood or even to their level of spiritual enlightenment or evolution. Thus, you'll hear people describe how you can raise your energy, by which they mean improve your mood, in order to align with your desires and manifest the life you want.

'Everything is energy, and that's all there is to it. Match the frequency of the reality you want, and you cannot help but get that reality. There can be no other way. This is not philosophy. This is physics.' -Darryl Anka

From this perspective, a 'high energy' person means a person who always acts from a state of alignment, or a heightened sense of awareness. These are people who have probably had a deep spiritual awakening and are beginning to view the world from a new perspective. They begin to see interconnectedness and oneness in all things and have consistent feelings of joy, bliss, love, and light that permeate every action they take.

LAW OF ATTRACTION

The ability to use energy to achieve a desired, intended effect— this is how I define the law of attraction. It is putting spirituality to use.

While the law of attraction has received quite a bit of attention in recent years, it is not a new concept. This idea has philosophical roots that date back to the early 19th-century approach known as "New Thought." There was a resurgence of interest in the idea during the 20th century, particularly with the 2006 release of the film "The Secret," which was later developed into the bestselling book of the same title and its 2010 sequel, "The Power." The law of attraction is a concept that holds that positive ideas produce positive events in one's life, while negative thoughts produce negative outcomes. It is founded on the notion that thoughts are a type of energy and that good energy attracts success in all aspects of life., including health, finances, and relationships.

Based on these lofty promises, it begs the question: Is the law of attraction real? While the law of attraction has gained popularity in recent years due to books like "The Secret," it lacks scientific evidence for its claims and is generally viewed as a pseudoscience.

How does the law of attraction work? Essentially, the energy of your thoughts manifests your experiences. So positive thoughts manifest positive experiences, and vice versa.

Advocates suggest there are three central universal principles that make up the law of attraction:

- Like attracts like: This law suggests that similar things are attracted to one another. It means that people tend to attract people who are similar to them, but it also suggests that people's thoughts tend to attract similar results. Negative thinking is believed to attract negative experiences, while positive thinking is believed to produce desirable experiences.

- Nature abhors a vacuum: This law of attraction suggests that removing negative things from your life can make space for more positive things to take their place. It is based on the notion that it is impossible to have a completely empty space in your mind and in your life. Since something will always fill this space, it is important to fill that space with positivity, proponents of this philosophy say.

- The present is always perfect: This law focuses on the idea that there are always things you can do to improve the present moment. While it might always seem like the present is somehow flawed, this law proposes that, rather than feeling dread or unhappiness, you should focus your energy on finding ways to make the present moment the best that it can be.

How to Use the Law of Attraction

So how do you get started with the law of attraction? According to this philosophy, you create your own reality. What you focus on is what you draw into your life. It suggests that what you believe will happen in your life is what does happen.

Some things that you can do to incorporate the law of attraction into your own life include:

- Be grateful
- Visualise your goals
- Look for the positives in a situation

- Learn how to identify negative thinking
- Use positive affirmations
- Reframe negative events in a more positive way

These buttress the point that energy is the life force that flows through all things. We can create anything we want with it because it is the wellspring of our power.

THE POWER OF VIBRATION

Vibration is the fundamental essence of the universe, governing everything from the smallest subatomic particles to the vast expanse of cosmic structures. It is the language of the universe, a harmonic resonance that underlies all existence. In this part, we will delve into the mysteries of vibration, exploring its role in shaping our reality and its potential to transform our lives.

The Science of Vibration

Vibration is a quantifiable phenomenon regulated by the principles of physics. Every object, thought, and emotion has a unique vibrational frequency, a signature that defines its essence. The vibrational frequency of an object is determined by its molecular structure, with each molecule oscillating at a specific rate. This oscillation creates a field of energy around the object, influencing its behaviour and interactions.

Vibration and Consciousness

Consciousness is a vibrational state, with thoughts and emotions manifesting at specific frequencies. By aligning our vibrational frequency with our desires, we can attract like energies and manifest our dreams. The power of vibration lies in its ability to reprogramme our consciousness, allowing us to tap into higher states of awareness and connect with the universe.

Practical Applications of Vibration

- Sound healing: utilising sound frequencies to balance and align energy.
- Meditation: focusing consciousness to resonate with higher frequencies.
- Manifestation: aligning vibrational frequency with desires to attract like energies.
- Energy work: manipulating vibrational frequencies

to balance and align energy.

In summary, vibration is the underlying force that shapes our reality. By understanding and harnessing the power of vibration, we can transform our lives, tap into higher states of consciousness, and connect with the universe. As we journey through the pages of this book, we will continue to explore the mysteries of vibration, unlocking its secrets and revealing its potential to revolutionise our understanding of the universe and prayer.

THE UNIVERSE AND NATURE: SYSTEMS, NOT CREATORS

Many have debated and explored the concept of God, or a higher power. Some individuals who do not subscribe to traditional religious beliefs often use terms such as the Universe, Nature, or Higher Power to describe a greater force. However, I believe that this is simply a substitute for the traditional concept of God and that the idea remains the same.

I do not believe in a creator who created the world and set it in motion. Instead, I see the Universe and Nature as systems that operate based on certain principles and laws. We must align ourselves with this system in order to achieve our goals and desires. Just as a farmer must align with the natural system to maximise his crop yield, we must align ourselves with the Universe and Nature to achieve our desires. This means understanding the principles and laws that govern the natural world and working in harmony with them.

Alignment with the Universe and Nature is not a matter of worship or religion, but rather a matter of understanding and working with the natural system. Just as a driver must understand the mechanics of a car to operate it effectively, we must understand the mechanics of the Universe and Nature to achieve our goals.

The Uniformity of Nature

The natural world operates with profound uniformity. Based on biology, a goat from the USA and a goat from Russia belong to the same species, just as an apple from

India and one from Nigeria come from the same species. This uniformity suggests that there is no creator who made the world and set it in motion. Instead, the Universe and Nature operate based on their own principles and laws.

I believe that the Universe and Nature are not a creator or higher power, but rather a system that we must align ourselves with in order to achieve our goals and desires. By understanding and working with the natural system, we can manifest our desires and create the life we want.

I do not accept the idea of a god or creator who brought the world into existence and set its course. If such a being had created the natural world, which we observe to be governed by uniform principles, it is reasonable to expect that it would have used the same uniformity to reveal itself to humanity. The fact that no such revelation has occurred leads me to conclude that there is no creator.

The Hidden Nature of a Supreme Being

Even if I were to consider the possibility of a supreme creator, it is clear that such a being has chosen to remain hidden and unknown. In this scenario, I believe it is futile to search for evidence of its existence, as it has apparently chosen not to reveal itself to us.

RELIGION

What about religion? Is there a right religion? Is there a religion that is better than another religion? Is there 'one true religion'?

There is this mindset in all human beings. No one wants to belong to the losing side. No one wants to be told that their choices are the wrong ones. People claim that their own religion is the right one. Even some of the texts of their scriptures also proclaim supremacy. And anyone who doesn't believe in or follow their religion is an unbeliever and is doomed to destruction. And each religious person seems to see himself or herself as wise and other people of other religions as foolish and wrong. In my own opinion, I see religion as a copy of previous religions that existed historically before it.

You cannot judge a fish's speed on land. You cannot judge a cheetah's speed in the water. Each animal has its own mechanism that is fit for its own habitat.

This is also how I see religion.

There is no right religion and no wrong religion. There is no good religion and no bad religion. There is no superior or inferior religion.

Each religion is in its own class. And what gives each religion its platform is its scriptures, or oral teachings passed down from antiquity.

You cannot use your own religion's scriptures to judge other religions. It is unwise. This is the error many religious followers commit.

They view their own as the best, superior, right, good, and sensible; and other folks' religions as garbage, wrong, bad, insensible, and barbaric.

It is the same value you have for your religion that others see in their own religion.

It is illogical to judge a fish's speed on the land, just as it is illogical to use your religion to judge other people's religion, no matter what is contained in your religion or that of another religion.

Every practitioner of a religion has their own personal

and authentic experience that is either established in their religion or convinced them to believe in their religion.

You cannot claim your experience is superior to others. The mere claim that people are converting to your religion is not proof of superiority. People are converting from one religion to another across different religions.

You cannot say your religion is more powerful than others. If you do your research, you will be amazed at more powerful practitioners of other religions doing outstanding miracles outside the ones written in your scriptures, and even any practitioner legend, dead or alive, that belonged to your religion.

Is water good or bad? Is fire good or bad? Is electricity good or bad? Is eating food good or bad? Are carnivorous animals feeding on other animals good or bad? Carnivorous animals have to feed. It is in their nature to kill. Does that make them good or bad?

Water is used to quench thirst, cook, wash and bathe. But the same water can cause flooding and drowning. Electricity powers different appliances but can cause fire that burns down buildings; it can electrocute.

There is no good or bad in nature.

This is how I evaluate religion. There is no good religion, and there is no bad religion.

Rather than expending our efforts on searching for the unknown or '*one true religion*', I believe we should focus on understanding and working with the natural system that we do know. By aligning ourselves with the principles and laws of the Universe and Nature, we can achieve our goals and desires without relying on the intervention of a creator.

Religion Vs. Spirituality

While religion and spirituality are related, there are differences between the two. Spirituality is an individual practice and belief, whereas religion is centred on a set of organised practices that a larger group shares. It is possible to be spiritual without being religious.

It is argued that it may be confusing to distinguish between spirituality and religion because of the ambiguous and personal meanings accorded to these concepts. Spirituality is a broad concept with many perspectives, and there is no consensus on a definition of this concept; there is only ambiguity as to how this concept is defined. Spirituality is an inherent component of being human, and it is subjective, intangible, and multifaceted.

Spirituality and religion are often used interchangeably, but the two concepts are different. Some authors contend that spirituality involves a personal quest for meaning in life, while religion involves an organised entity with rituals and practices focusing on a higher power, or God. Spirituality may be related to religion for certain individuals, but not, for example, for an atheist or yoga practitioner.

Similarly, some authors contend that spirituality refers to the '*nearly universal human search for meaning, often involving some sense of transcendence.*' On the other hand, religion is '*a set of beliefs, practices, and language that characterises a community that is searching for transcendent meaning in a particular way, generally based upon belief in a deity.*' Spirituality and religion can take individual as well as collective forms. The concepts of spirituality and religiosity are not mutually exclusive and can overlap or exist separately. However, prayer and meditation are often performed in solitude. Regular church attendance, religious belief, or the influence of religious institutions have been dwindling fast in recent years, and there is also a tendency for people to believe without belonging to any religious affiliation in Western Europe and much of the developed world, irrespective of race and ethnicity. *Crockett & Voas* further assert that there is a generational decline in belief as well as religious belonging and attendance in Western Europe and much of the developed world. On the other hand, in sub-Saharan Africa, many people still believe in and belong to spiritual or religious institutions, and religious plurality is common.

Weathers et al. give a conceptual definition of spirituality as 'a way of being in the world in which a person feels a sense of connectedness to themselves, others, and/or a higher power of nature; a sense of meaning in life; and transcendence beyond self, everyday living, and suffering.'

In contrast, *Kaplan and Wood* hold that spirituality is more than prayer, meditation, contemplation, or personal reflection. It gives a sense of meaning to everyday life.

However, these scholars further assert that religion and spirituality have received increased interest in relation to serious illnesses in recent years. *Chaves* conceptualised spirituality as support, relationship with the sacred, and transcendence. He also distinguished spirituality from religion, which is defined by religious affiliation, cultural affiliation, and dogmas.

As previous research has shown, religion and spirituality are related but distinct. Religiosity refers to the institutional and interpersonal engagement with a formal religious group, its doctrines, and its traditions. In contrast, spirituality is one's sense of interconnectedness with a transcendent being (spiritual perceptions).

For the purpose of this study, our working definition of Spirituality is *'personal belief in God or a Higher Power, that may include individual prayer, meditation, and meaning in Self,'* and Religion is defined as *'organisational beliefs or adherence to institutionally based belief systems or dogmas.'*

With reference to these definitions, we aim to reduce the line between spirituality and religion, especially as some phenomena associated with spirituality are essential elements of a broad conceptualization of religion.

You may have heard—or even used—the terms religion and spirituality interchangeably. But while they aren't diametric opposites, neither are they the same. Learn how to tell the difference between religion and spirituality.

For thousands of years, humanity has passionately pursued the truth with a capital T—the ultimate answers to life and the universe. This perennial knowledge constitutes the answers to what are often called the soul questions:

- Who am I?
- What do I want?
- What is my purpose?
- What is the meaning of life?

Historically, from the perspective of the soul, there have been two foundational routes to discovering these truths: religion and spirituality. Although they have many similarities and there is a relationship between the two, there are differences between religion and spirituality.

Religion: By definition, *religion* is a personal set or institutionalised system of religious attitudes, beliefs, and practices; it is the service and worship of God or the supernatural.

Spirituality: *Spirituality*, on the other hand, connotes an experience of connection to something larger than you; living everyday life in a reverent and sacred manner. Or as Christina Puchalski, MD (leader in trying to incorporate spirituality into healthcare), puts it, *'Spirituality is the aspect of humanity that refers to the way individuals seek and express meaning and purpose and the way they experience their connectedness to the moment, to self, to others, to nature, and to the significant or sacred.'*[8]

PART FIVE: PRAYING WITH ENERGY

VIBRATIONAL POWER OF PRAYER

'I found that when you start thinking and saying what you really want, then your mind automatically shifts and pulls you in that direction. And sometimes it can be that simple—just a little twist in vocabulary that illustrates your attitude and philosophy.'
JIM ROHN

Prayer is not a ritual or a routine, but a deliberate act with a specific intention. It is not enough to simply pray without expectation or purpose. We must approach prayer with a clear desire and intention, seeking a specific outcome.

My followers around the world have witnessed the remarkable results of purposeful prayer. I have seen people afflicted with incurable diseases, including cancer and HIV, receive instant healing. Doctors have been left stunned and perplexed, unable to explain the sudden and complete recovery. I have also prayed for people's businesses, relationships, careers, and families and seen instant and total turnarounds. Businesses have received contracts worth millions and billions of dollars, and individuals have experienced breakthroughs that have changed their lives forever.

The key to activating the vibrational power of prayer is not just about reciting words or following a formula. It is about approaching prayer with a clear intention, a specific purpose, and a deep understanding of the natural laws that govern our universe. When we pray with purpose and intention, we tap into the powerful forces that shape our reality. I have discovered the power of making purposeful declarations.

My words have brought instant transformation to people's lives, without the need for lengthy prayers or rituals. I can declare, "*Stand up and walk*," and the lame shall rise. I can say, "*Check your body, it is gone*," and diseases shall vanish. I can proclaim, "*Receive financial breakthrough*," and abundance shall flow. I can simply say, "*It is done*," or "*You are free*," and a multitude of testimonies shall erupt, testifying to the power of my word.

This is through the activation of the vibrational power of prayer which I call *Praying With Energy*'.

Praying with Energy

Through over 21 years of spiritual growth and exploration, I have developed a unique and effective approach to prayer, which I call 'Praying with Energy.' This technique has consistently demonstrated its capacity to bring desires into manifestation, and I am excited to share it with you.

'Praying with Energy' is a powerful methodology that combines the principles of spiritual connection, focused intention, and energetic alignment to bring about desired outcomes. By harnessing the energy of our thoughts, emotions, and beliefs, we can create a vibrational resonance that attracts what we seek to manifest.

HOW TO ACTIVATE THE VIBRATIONAL POWER OF PRAYER

To activate the vibrational power of prayer, which will help you get what you want, you need to follow the steps in the 'Praying with Energy' process.

❖ Step 1: Define Your Desire with Clarity and Belief

To effectively pray with energy, you must first define your desire with precision and clarity. Be specific and detailed about what you want to manifest. For instance, if your desire is a car, specify the make, model, year, colour, and whether you want a new or used vehicle.

It is crucial to ensure that your desires align with your beliefs and values. Your mind must be able to conceive and believe in the possibility of achieving your desire. If your desire seems too far-fetched or doubtful, your mind will struggle to believe it, making manifestation impossible.

If the concept of manifesting ten trillion pounds within twenty-four hours is not aligned with my beliefs and mental framework, then my mind is unable to conceive and internalise such a vast amount in such a short timeframe. This is a crucial prerequisite for manifestation, as the mind plays a vital role in shaping our reality. I cannot envision a scenario where this amount materialises without a genuine belief in its possibility.

In cases where your desire stretches your belief limits, it is essential to train your mind to embrace the possibility. Engage in activities that foster belief, such as reading inspiring stories, watching motivational videos, or participating in empowering workshops. Surround yourself with positive influences that nurture your beliefs and confidence.

Remember, belief is the foundation of manifestation. By cultivating a strong belief in your desire, you set the stage for the next steps in the 'Praying with Energy' process.

❖   Step 2: Meditate—Visualise Your Desire with Clarity

Meditation is a powerful tool for manifesting our desires. My definition of meditation is the intentional focus of our thoughts on a specific outcome, visualising it as already achieved. During meditation, I create vivid mental scenarios that bring my desire to life. For instance, when I desired to own a Range Rover, I collected images and videos of the exact model I wanted, depicting its interior, exterior, and even someone driving it. This visualisation exercise enabled me to imagine myself behind the wheel, holding the keys, and experiencing the joy of ownership.

To meditate effectively:

- ➤ Imagine yourself already in possession of your desire.
- ➤ Create sensory experiences, such as sights, sounds, and emotions.
- ➤ Repeat this process until your thoughts feel as real as the actual experience.
- ➤ Practice meditation anywhere, at any time, in a comfortable posture.

Through regular meditation, you can tap into the energy

of your thoughts, aligning your vibration with the frequency of your desire. This alignment is crucial for successful manifestation.

Initially, you may struggle to conjure a vivid mental image or summon a strong thought. However, with consistent practice, you'll reach a point where your thoughts become almost palpable, feeling as real as if the desired outcome has already materialised. This is a crucial milestone, as it signifies that your vibrational frequency has aligned with that of your desired outcome, enabling manifestation.

Your thoughts possess the power of energy, and harnessing this energy is essential for effective manifestation. To facilitate this process, incorporate meditation into your daily routine, utilising techniques that resonate with you, such as music, nature, or personal reflection. Feel free to adapt your approach to suit your individual needs and comfort level, sans rigid adherence to traditional postures or settings.

It's important to note that meditation doesn't require specific physical postures, such as sitting with legs crossed in a lotus position. Instead, prioritise comfort and relaxation in your chosen position. Avoid any poses that may cause physical discomfort or pain. Feel free to adapt a stance that suits your individual needs, whether that means standing, sitting, taking a walk, or even lying down. The goal is to cultivate a relaxed and calm state, allowing your mind to focus on your desired outcome.

❖ Step 3: Affirm - Harnessing the Power of Positive Declarations

Affirmations are powerful statements that, when spoken, tap into the energy of sound to manifest our desires. To affirm means to proclaim your desired outcomes, either during or after meditation. This step helps rewire your mind with positive thoughts, aligning your vibration with your goals.

Craft personalised affirmations that resonate with your

aspirations, such as:

- I am already successful!
- I have abundance!
- Life always works in my favour!
- I enjoy good health!
- I am worthy of love and respect!
- I trust in my abilities!
- I am grateful for all I have!

Remember:

- Repeat your affirmations regularly, especially when you feel stressed or doubtful.
- Believe in the truth of your affirmations, even if they don't feel true yet.
- Use present-tense language, as if your desires have already come true.
- Focus on what you want, rather than what you don't want.
- Be patient and consistent, as affirmations

are a powerful tool for long-term transformation.

Incorporate positive speech into your daily life, whether in conversations or solo reflections. Consistently thinking and speaking positively attracts positive experiences, so refrain from negative self-talk and focus on affirming your desires.

The power of speech is a formidable force in shaping our reality. When we utter words, we release sound energy that resonates in our lives. This energy attracts corresponding experiences, manifesting as positive or negative outcomes. By consciously choosing to speak positively, we create a magnetic field that draws good things towards us.

Conversely, negative words perpetuate harmful energy, hindering our potential for growth and success.

Recognising the significance of spoken words, it's essential to mind our language and cultivate a habit of positive speech. By doing so, we can:

- Attract abundance and prosperity.
- Foster healthy relationships.
- Enhance our well-being.
- Boost confidence and self-esteem.
- Create a positive environment

Remember, the energy of our words has a profound impact on our lives. Let us harness the power of positive speech to shape our destiny and manifest our desires.

❖ Step 4: Take Proactive Steps of Faith

When you've completed steps 1-3, your mind may receive intuitive guidance on actions to take, directions to pursue, and people to connect with to facilitate your manifestation. Inspiration can come through various channels, such as:

- Intuition.
- Dreams.
- Advice from others.

- Personal reflections

To prepare for your desired outcome, take proactive steps like:

- Acquiring new skills or qualifications.
- Volunteering or taking on related projects.
- Networking and building connections.

By doing so, you position yourself for success and increase your chances of manifesting your desire. For instance, if you're seeking employment, enhance your resume and online profiles, and engage in activities that demonstrate your expertise.

Real-life examples illustrate the power of taking steps of faith:

- ❖ I am delighted to share a testimonial from one of my followers in Dubai, who had been facing a challenging period of unemployment as an expatriate for six months. Following a prayer session, he chose to trust his intuition and visited an office without any advertised vacancies. With faith and confidence, he declared, 'You have a job for me.' This bold step marked the end of his joblessness, as he successfully secured employment. This testimony highlights the power of faith and intuition in manifesting positive outcomes.

- ❖ Another remarkable testimonial comes from a follower who was facing financial difficulties. After watching my videos, she experienced a moment of inspiration, recognising an untapped opportunity in her own backyard. She had an abundance of a specific vegetable in her garden, which she did not realise was in high demand but unmet in the market. Seizing this insight, she took swift action and brought her produce to the market, selling out within an impressive one-hour timeframe. This innovative approach has since become a lucrative venture for her, generating consistent income.

You can access more inspiring testimonials like this on my TikTok and YouTube channels, showcasing the transformative power of faith, intuition, and proactive action in manifesting success and prosperity

Testimonies like these demonstrate the importance of proactive faith in manifesting desires. Embrace the power of taking steps towards your goals, and recognise that your efforts are essential to making your miracles happen.

Debunking the Myth of Special Prayer Times

I disagree with the notion that prayers are more effective at specific times or dates. Prayer is personal, unaffected by clock time or calendar dates. However, I acknowledge that intuition can play a crucial role in identifying opportune moments for prayer.

Feel free to choose any time that suits you for prayer, but

remain attuned to your intuition. When guided to pray at a specific time or period, trust that the energy vibrations are aligning in favour of your desires. By honouring your inner wisdom, you can harness the power of aligned energy, amplifying the impact of your prayers.

Nature operates in cycles, with energy fluctuations occurring throughout the day, week, or month. Intuition can help tap into these vibrational shifts, allowing us to align our prayers with the optimal energy frequency. This synchronisation can enhance the potency of our prayers, facilitating manifestation.

PART SIX: LIGHT LANGUAGE

THE LANGUAGE OF ENERGY

'When you become the master of your mind, you are the master of everything.'

SWAMI SATCHIDANANDA

Light language is a channelled multidimensional language that brings sound and energy from the spirit into the physical. It is a form of sound healing that can help us connect with higher realms of consciousness. It can be expressed through the voice (singing, toning, chanting, or speaking), hands (writing or drawing), or body (movement/intuitive hand gestures).

Light language communicates to the soul. It is not something you have to understand with the human mind; it is rather something you feel deep inside of your heart. It brings through powerful vibrations and codes that support us to process shifts in consciousness, release deeply held blockages, and bring us in touch with our truth. It is here to awaken and activate. It is here to assist in the ascension process and raise the consciousness of humanity. It is truly one of the most powerful healing tools I have experienced, and I am beyond grateful to share it with you. [9]

Light Language is a form of communication that bypasses human limitations around the meaning of words. As opposed to a language made up of symbols and sounds that we have mutually agreed upon as a society or culture, Light Language has no fixed alphabet. It is a vibrational expression that speaks directly to our soul and DNA.

The purpose of Light Language is to shift our energy to a higher frequency than we usually inhabit. It helps our brains enter the receptivity of the gamma state, which connects multiple areas of our brain. Gamma waves are associated with increased memory recall, sensory perception, focus, processing speed, and creativity. Light language can be spoken, written, transmitted through binaural beats, danced, signed with the hands, or toned. It is as individual as each channel that brings it through. [10]

THE LANGUAGE OF ENERGY: Unlocking the Power of Light Language

I believe that Light language, also known as speaking in tongues or speaking in the spirit, is a powerful form of communication that transcends human understanding. This phenomenon, familiar to Christians, enables individuals to speak in a language they have not learned, which may sound like gibberish to the untrained ear. However, I refer to it as the Language of Energy, as it harmonises us with nature and releases energy into specific areas of our lives in ways beyond our comprehension.

By tapping into our intuitive abilities, we can decipher the meaning behind our Light Language expressions, unlocking a deeper understanding of the wisdom and guidance we receive. This extraordinary language has the potential to revolutionise our connection with the world around us and unlock new dimensions of personal growth and transformation.

Should You Incorporate Light Language into Your Prayers? My Stance

While I don't advocate for the necessity of speaking in Light Language, I acknowledge its potential benefits as a personal choice in prayer. This unique form of communication may serve as a means to access nature's energy, potentially preempting unforeseen challenges or mitigating the effects of negative events on our lives and loved ones.

Just as nature has its inherent sounds—a baby's cry, an animal's call— Light Language taps into this primal expression. By incorporating it into our prayers, we harness nature's energy to infuse positive vibrations into our lives, often beyond our conscious understanding.

Personally, I occasionally speak in Light Language when inspired to do so, embracing the intuitive guidance and energetic resonance it provides.

Guidelines for Speaking Light Language:

- Cultivate belief in your ability to speak Light Language.
- Create a conducive environment that fosters spiritual awareness and concentration. This may involve playing uplifting music or sounds that resonate with your spiritual nature.
- Attune yourself to the intense spiritual atmosphere, syncing with its flow.
- Open your mouth in faith, intending to speak Light Language.
- Verbalise any inspired vocabulary that comes to mind. If none arises, pronounce any words that come to you, trusting they hold significance.

Remember, what may seem like gibberish to the untrained ear is actually a powerful, intuitive language. Don't worry if you don't speak Light Language immediately; with patience and consistent practice, you'll eventually tap into its flow.

Interpreting Light Language: A Step-by-Step Guide

- Cultivate a calm and serene state of mind.
- Speak in Light Language, allowing the words to flow freely.
- Pay attention to any inspired thoughts that arise during or after speaking. These thoughts hold the meaning and interpretation of your Light Language expression.
- If no inspired thoughts emerge immediately, remain calm and relaxed. Avoid anxiety or panic, and instead, allow your mind to settle into a receptive state.
- As you enter this contemplative state, your mind will begin to receive intuitive insights and understanding. Be patient, as this process may take time.

Remember, interpreting Light Language is a skill that develops with practice and spiritual attunement. Don't worry if understanding doesn't come immediately. With persistence and patience, you'll eventually tap into the wisdom and guidance contained within your Light Language expressions.

PART SEVEN: UNDERSTANDING PRAYER BLOCKAGES

THE IMPACT OF NEGATIVE ENERGY AND TIMING

"Whatever we plant in our subconscious mind and nourish with repetition and emotion will one day become a reality."
EARL NIGHTINGALE

In our spiritual journey, we often encounter obstacles that hinder the manifestation of our prayers. As I have established earlier, the answer to prayer is dependent on us. We are solely responsible for answering our prayers. However, there are instances where our prayers may seem to go unanswered. In this part, we will explore the two primary factors that can block our prayers: Negative Energy and Timing.

NEGATIVE ENERGY - THE UNSEEN BARRIER

Negative energy is a formidable obstacle that can prevent our prayers from manifesting. These internal barriers can repel or neutralise the positive energy we attempt to manifest, making it essential to address and release them.

Negative energy is a profound hindrance to prayer manifestation, encompassing various forms, including:

- Limiting beliefs and thoughts of lack.
- Unbelief and doubt.
- Negative affirmations.
- Generational curses or inherited patterns of negativity.
- Harmful charms, spells, or hexes.
- Beliefs and patterns perpetuating bad luck or destiny

These diverse forms of negative energy can:

- Repel positive energy and blessings.
- Attract unwanted circumstances.
- Reinforce self-doubt and limitation.
- Hinder spiritual growth and progress

Recognising and addressing these manifestations of negative energy is crucial to releasing their hold and fostering a conducive environment for prayer manifestation.

GENERATIONAL CURSES: A MANIFESTATION OF NEGATIVE ENERGY

Generational curses, also known as ancestral curses, are spiritual patterns that perpetuate negative energy through family lines, influencing an individual's life and manifestation. Just as physical DNA is passed down from parents, spiritual properties can also be inherited. These curses can manifest as recurring patterns, such as:

- Marriage difficulties or divorce.
- Premature death at a specific age.
- Financial struggles.
- Chronic illnesses

To break free from these cycles, it is essential to address and release the negative energy through self-deliverance or seek the guidance of a spiritual master. By doing so, you can:

- Terminate the legal flow of the curse's effect on your bloodline.

- Liberate yourself and future generations from its grip.
- Restore your spiritual inheritance, enabling effortless manifestation.

Remember, awareness and action are key to shattering the hold of generational curses, spells, charms and unlocking your full potential.

THE IMPORTANCE OF ENERGY CLEANSING

Just as a vehicle requires regular maintenance to ensure optimal performance, our aura requires periodic cleansing to remove accumulated negative energy. Constant use of our aura can lead to energetic buildup, hindering our spiritual and emotional well-being.

Energy cleansing is essential to remove negative energy residue, restore aura balance and harmony, enhance spiritual and emotional resilience, and improve overall well-being.

Regular cleansing is crucial to maintaining a healthy, vibrant aura, allowing us to navigate life's challenges with greater ease and manifest our desires with greater success.

TIMING - THE NATURE SCHEDULE

The universe operates on its own rhythm and schedule, often prioritising long-term growth and learning over instant gratification. Nature timing may not always align with our immediate expectations, requiring us to cultivate patience and trust in the manifestation process.

Nature's Timeline

The natural world operates on a predetermined timeline, where progression unfolds in a sequential and orderly manner. Illustrative examples include:

- Seeds requiring time to germinate and mature into trees.

- Human gestation lasting approximately nine months.
- Children developing into adults through a gradual process.
- Seasons transitioning in a predictable and cyclical pattern.

These examples demonstrate that nature does not rush or accelerate growth but rather adheres to an intrinsic schedule. Similarly, our lives and endeavours are subject to this principle, emphasising the importance of patience and allowing things to unfold in their own time.

Individual Variations in Growth and Development
Nature's processes are governed by inherent timing, which accommodates individual differences. A striking example is the onset of puberty, where a group of boys born on the same day will reach this milestone at different ages. Some will be early bloomers, while others, like myself, will be late bloomers, reaching puberty at 17. This variation is

attributed to unique genetic structures, resulting in diverse body compositions that influence growth rates. Despite these differences, we all ultimately reach adulthood, illustrating nature's flexible and accommodating timing.

Just as unique genetic structures affect growth and development, they also shape the immune system's response to pathogens and diseases. As a result, some individuals' immune systems are naturally stronger and more resilient, while others may be more susceptible to illnesses. This genetic variability is a natural aspect of human biology, highlighting the importance of personalised approaches to health and wellness.

The human immune system is highly variable between individuals but relatively stable over time within a given person. Recent conceptual and technological advances have enabled systems immunology analyses, which reveal the composition of immune cells and proteins in populations of healthy individuals. The range of variation and some specific influences that shape an individual's immune system is now becoming clearer. Human immune systems vary as a consequence of heritable and non-heritable influences, but symbiotic and pathogenic microbes and other non-heritable influences explain most of this variation.[11]

Aligning with the Universe's Timeline

When our desires seem delayed, it's essential to consider the universe's timing. Sometimes, we must wait for the optimal moment for our desires to manifest. However, there are instances where we can set a reasonable timeframe for manifestation, aligning our energy with the desired outcome.

To manifest our desires, we must raise our vibration to match the level of what we seek. This can be achieved through intense meditation, affirmations, and fasting (optional).

By elevating our energy, we create a resonance that attracts our desires, aligning with the universe's timing. This harmonisation is crucial for successful manifestation. Remember, patience and trust in the universe's plan are vital. When our energy and timing align, manifestation becomes a natural outcome.

Overcoming Prayer Blockages

To overcome these obstacles, we must:

- Identify and release negative energy patterns.
- Align our energy with our desires.
- Cultivate patience and trust in universe's (nature's) timing

By understanding and addressing these prayer blockages, we can refine our prayer practice, enhance our spiritual growth, and manifest our desires with greater ease and grace.

PART EIGHT: GRATITUDE

GRATITUDE: PRAYER WITH VIBRATIONAL POWER

'The more you recognise and express gratitude for the things you have, the more things you will have to express gratitude for.'
ZIG ZAGLAR

Gratitude, especially when expressed through prayer, holds vibrational power that can transform your life.

Prayer of Gratitude is a practice that allows you to shift your focus from problems to blessings. Regularly affirming gratitude and meditating on blessings can train your mind to focus on the positive, even in difficult circumstances.

Learn to appreciate your current circumstances, progress, and achievements. Avoid fixating on what's lacking, and instead, celebrate your small victories and accomplishments. This mindset maintains positive energy and releases it into the universe, strengthening your belief system and paving the way for future desires to manifest.

Focusing on the Positive

Don't be overwhelmed by what you don't have. Instead, be thankful for what you already possess, as you await the manifestation of your desires. Gratitude for your current blessings sets the stage for future manifestations.

Anticipatory Gratitude

Be thankful for the future manifestation of your desires, as if they have already occurred. This proactive gratitude aligns your energy with your desires, drawing them closer to reality.

By embracing gratitude, you'll attract more positive energy, reinforce your belief system, and align yourself with the universe's abundance, leading to the successful manifestation of your desires.

Gratitude is one of the healthiest emotions you can experience, and practicing gratitude is a powerful tool when you want to manifest your dreams and goals.

Manifestation is based on the universal law of attraction; we attract what we focus on. So, we better focus on the things for which we are grateful. In this book, I share all my tips on how to use the power of gratitude in your manifestations.

Benefits of Gratitude

Let's discuss the benefits of gratitude, especially when combined with the law of attraction, and how you can use the vibrating power of gratitude to start manifesting all your heart's desires. I will also cover things like the effects of gratitude on the brain and how practicing it daily can truly change your life and give you more joy

The power of gratitude has only just begun to be thoroughly researched, and we are continuously discovering its countless benefits.

I personally believe that gratitude is the most powerful manifesting method for reaching your big dreams and goals.

It's like showing the universe, day in and day out, what it should deliver: just the things you are grateful for, all the stuff that makes you happy.

If you're feeling a bit stuck at the moment, or if you're ready and excited to elevate your life, then learning how to practice gratitude is one of the best places to start.
Not only will it create more health and happiness in your life, but you will also have a much easier time manifesting what you want.
So, there are many reasons to feel gratitude every day!

Effects Of Gratitude On The Brain
Some of the effects of gratitude on the brain include decreased stress, emotional regulation, and an increased likelihood of positive emotion.

The better you are feeling physically and emotionally, the easier it is for you to realise your dreams and take the necessary action to reach your goals.

Reduced Stress

Practicing gratitude reduces stress by focusing attention on something that enhances your life—all the things that make your life more joyful.

It releases your mind from the bonds of negative emotions that may have you feeling trapped.

For example, if you are worried about a lack of money, you may be feeling the stress of living close to the edge. But if you take some time to focus on one thing you have, something that you can be grateful for (good health, a strong relationship, a community you're a part of), it can change your perspective and release the emotions of '*having*' instead of 'not having'.

When we feel in our minds that our needs are met (even if they aren't yet), it sends a signal to our brain that we can relax and exit fight or flight mode.

Refocusing our attention from just 'hope' to the feeling of 'it has already happened', exactly the state we are in when we feel gratitude relieves the pressure we feel on an emotional and mental level.

When we do this continuously, it becomes more accessible as the brain follows the habits that we teach it.

Emotional Regulation

In terms of increasing emotional regulation, gratitude works by increasing activity in your pre-frontal cortex. This is the area of the brain where both the right and left hemispheres meet. It lights up when we experience social situations and pleasure.

Increasing neural activity in this section of the brain causes new positive neurons to fire. When you do this repeatedly, the capacity for more similar activities increases. The brain begins to expect this type of activity.

With the increase in positive activity in the pre-frontal cortex, your emotional regulation system is stronger and healthier, allowing you to have a much better grip on your emotions.

Increased Likelihood Of Positive Emotion
Brain researchers have shown that you can rewire your brain over time. In simple terms, *'neurons that fire together, wire together'*.

That means that the more you practise specific thoughts and behaviours, the stronger the connections will be between those thoughts and actions.
This is also a powerful tool for manifestation.

So, when you practise gratitude and feel these enjoyable, stress-relieving, peace-inducing emotions, your ability to do it more and more increases.

If you consciously practise gratitude daily, soon, your brain will be looking for reasons to experience gratitude without you telling it to.

The Power Of Gratitude For Manifesting

Now that we know a little bit more about how gratitude affects us physically and emotionally, let's talk about the power of gratitude and how it helps you manifest faster.

Gratitude is helpful for manifestation because it creates a state of abundance within us and changes our mindset.

By merely focusing on the things we are grateful for in our lives, we create an understanding that we are provided for, we are safe, and we have plenty.

This is a very powerful abundance message you'll send to your subconscious mind.

When talking about manifestation, vibrational frequencies and alignment are important. Since everything in our world is made of energy, it carries an energetic frequency, similar to that of a radio transmitter. We are only ever able to 'tune' into the frequencies at which we operate.

For instance, if you continually feel stress, lack, or shame, you are running on a frequency that is in tune with those emotions and thoughts.

In other words, you are telling your subconscious that *THIS* is your reality.

When you're tuned to the frequency of joy, abundance, and, most importantly, gratitude, then you're attracting more of it.

When you are tuned to higher frequencies through emotions like gratitude, acceptance, love, and abundance, you have changed your tune to match that of the feelings you're looking to feel.

So when you're tuned to the right frequencies, you attract what's on that level.

Gratitude is the emotional signature of receiving. By remaining in the state of receiving, you are matching your frequency with already having what you desire.

Even if you consciously understand you haven't received it yet, feeling gratitude keeps your energetic vibration at the level of abundance and sends this message to your subconscious, thus attracting what you want.

Use Gratitude To Clear Abundance Blocks And Negative Emotions.

To manifest more abundance in your life, you need to clear some of your manifestation blocks. These blocks can include limiting beliefs, negative emotions, or even bad habits.

They can be built up from internal beliefs that you are not worthy of abundance and that you are not able to truly manifest your dreams.

However, practicing gratitude for the things you want but haven't yet received can put you into the emotional state of already having what you want.

This is like bringing your future goal into your present life with a very easy trick: you just have to say thanks for it! (What an amazing manifestation trick, isn't it?)

The more your mind becomes familiar with these emotions, the more it lets go of past thinking patterns of unworthiness and accepts your new way of thinking as the new normal.

Gratitude + Generosity = Abundance

One of my favourite formulae for manifestation success is gratitude plus generosity results in abundance.

This is incredibly powerful for two reasons:
- ➢ Practicing gratitude already signals to your brain that you have what you want.
- ➢ By being generous with what you have, it doubles

down on your faith that you are abundant and have plenty to spare.

Generosity is your real-world 'proof' that you genuinely believe that you are abundant.

When you believe strongly enough to take action through generosity, then you are absolutely aligned with abundance.

How To Practice Gratitude Consistently

There are many ways to cultivate a feeling of gratitude in your life. This is because it is an emotion, and humans can create emotion in their minds and bodies through thought alone.

By thinking about things you are grateful for, you are automatically practicing gratitude. Just try to think about the person or people in your life for whom you are most thankful for and feel the wave of positive emotion wash over you.

❖ Have a Gratitude Journal

The simplest way to practice gratitude is to make a list of things you are thankful for every day. This manifesting technique is called a gratitude list or gratitude journal.

You can do this on a piece of paper or mentally, though it is more powerful if you write it down. Every day, write down three to five things you are grateful for. When you write them down, focus on why you're thankful and spend some time focusing solely on being thankful without expectation.

For example, one day, you may be grateful for a healthy breakfast, a good sleep, and a supportive partner. Next, you may be thankful for the gift of sight, a positive memory, or a passion you share.

It doesn't matter how big or small the thing you're

grateful for is. As long as you create the emotion, you're on the right track.

You can also write thank-you notes to people whom you appreciate. Someone who has been there for you through a tough time. Someone who you admire and who has impacted your life. Or someone who needs a little bit of encouragement...

If you write down grateful thoughts towards a person, even if you do not send the note, it creates a sense of well-being and wholeness in your body.

❖ Do Something Selfless

Another way to practice gratitude is to do something selfless. You could give to charity, offer help to someone who needs it, buy the person in line behind you a coffee...

When you do something selfless, it creates a sense of togetherness and gratitude within you that you can have a positive impact on another person's life.

The critical thing to remember is that consistency is key!

You experience the benefits of gratitude the moment you feel it. However, when you cause yourself to enter a state of gratitude regularly, you experience the benefits over and over again.

Continuous gratitude will have a compound effect. The gratitude you practice today will positively impact you for weeks to come.

That means, when you are practicing gratitude in those coming weeks, you will experience the residual benefits and the immediate benefits of appreciation, causing a positivity snowball effect that grows stronger and bigger as you practise.[12]

CONCLUSION

Prayer is a powerful tool for manifesting desires, akin to meditation and affirmations.

It is crucial to recognise that individual responsibility plays a vital role in manifestation, necessitating inspired action and alignment with natural principles.

Time and posture are mere formalities, as the essence of prayer lies in vibrational resonance.

Periodic clearance of negative energy is essential to maintain a conducive vibrational state, ensuring the attraction of desired outcomes.

When these principles are embraced and applied, manifestation becomes an inevitability. As you apply these principles, remember that patience and trust are vital.

Your desires will manifest in due time, and your testimonies will be a testament to the power of prayer and the universe's alignment.

I eagerly anticipate hearing testimonies of transformation and success as you integrate these principles into your life.

Feel free to share your experiences via WhatsApp or during my live sessions on TikTok.

May your journey be guided by the wisdom of nature and the power of prayer.

QUESTION AND ANSWER SECTION

Welcome to the Q&A section of "The Vibrational Power of Prayer," where we'll delve deeper into the topics discussed earlier, exploring additional facets and offering practical advice to enhance your understanding and experience of the vibrational power of prayer.

Q: What is the vibrational power of prayer?
A: The vibrational power of prayer refers to the ability of our thoughts, emotions, and intentions to shape our reality and attract positive energy into our lives.

Q: How does prayer work?
A: Prayer works by aligning our energy with the universal energy that connects us all, allowing us to manifest our desires, overcome challenges, and cultivate inner peace.

Q: What is the difference between traditional prayer and vibrational prayer?
A: Traditional prayer often focuses on asking a higher power for help, while vibrational prayer focuses on aligning our energy with the universe to manifest our desires.

Q: **How can I practice vibrational prayer?**
A: You can practice vibrational prayer by setting intentions, visualising your desires, and cultivating a positive mindset, while also using techniques like meditation, affirmations, and gratitude.

Q: **What are the benefits of vibrational prayer?**
A: The benefits of vibrational prayer include manifesting our desires, overcoming challenges, cultivating inner peace, and developing a deeper connection with ourselves and the world around us.

Q: **Can anyone practice vibrational prayer?**
A: Yes, anyone can practice vibrational prayer, regardless of their spiritual beliefs or background. It is a universal tool that can be used by anyone to improve their life.

Q: **How long does it take to see results from vibrational prayer?**
A: Results from vibrational prayer can vary depending on the individual and their circumstances. Some people may see immediate results, while others may need to practice consistently over time to see changes in their lives.

Q: **How can I overcome doubts and fears when practicing** vibrational prayer?

A: You can overcome doubts and fears by cultivating a positive mindset, focusing on gratitude, and trusting in the universe's plan. Remember, vibrational prayer is a journey, and it's normal to encounter challenges along the way.

Q: How can I use vibrational prayer to manifest my desires?

A: To manifest your desires, focus on visualising what you want to create, setting and cultivating a positive mindset. Use affirmations and gratitude to align your energy with your desires.

Q: Can vibrational prayer help me overcome challenges?

A: Yes, vibrational prayer can help you overcome challenges by aligning your energy with the universe and attracting positive solutions. Focus on letting go of fear and doubt.

Q: How does vibrational prayer relate to the law of attraction?

A: Vibrational prayer is a powerful tool for manifesting your desires, which is a key principle of the law of attraction. By aligning your energy with the universe, you can attract what you want into your life.

Q: Can I use vibrational prayer for others?

A: Yes, you can use vibrational prayer for others by focusing on their highest good and visualising positive outcomes. This can be a powerful way to support loved ones and contribute to the greater good.

Q: **How can I incorporate vibrational prayer into my daily life?**
A: You can incorporate vibrational prayer into your daily life by setting aside time each day to practice, using reminders to stay focused, and applying the principles to your daily actions and decisions.

Q14: **Is the myth of special prayer times real?**
A: I disagree with the notion that prayers are more effective at specific times or dates. Prayer is personal, unaffected by clock time or calendar dates. However, I acknowledge that intuition can play a crucial role in identifying opportune moments for prayer.

Q: **What role does gratitude play in vibrational prayer?**
A: Gratitude is a powerful catalyst for vibrational prayer, as it helps align your energy with the universe and attract positive experiences. Focus on cultivating gratitude for what you already have and what you want to create.

Q: **Can vibrational prayer help me develop a deeper spiritual connection?**

A: Yes, vibrational prayer can help you develop a deeper spiritual connection by aligning your energy with the universe and cultivating a sense of oneness. Regular practice can help you feel more connected to yourself, others, and the world around you.

Q: **How can I overcome negative thoughts and emotions when practicing vibrational prayer?**

A: To overcome negative thoughts and emotions, focus on acknowledging and releasing them, then shift your attention to positive thoughts and emotions that align with your desires.

Q: **Can vibrational prayer be used for physical healing?**

A: Yes, vibrational prayer can be used for physical healing by focusing on visualising perfect health, cultivating a positive mindset, and aligning your energy with the universe.

Q: **How can I use vibrational prayer to manifest abundance?**

A: To manifest abundance, focus on visualising prosperity, cultivating a mindset of gratitude and abundance, and aligning your energy with the universe.

Q: **Can vibrational prayer be used in conjunction with other spiritual practices?**

A: Yes, vibrational prayer can be used in conjunction with other spiritual practices like meditation, yoga, and affirmations to enhance their effectiveness.

Q: **How can I know if my vibrational prayer is working?**

A: You can know if your vibrational prayer is working by paying attention to synchronicities, feeling shifts in your energy and mood, and seeing positive changes in your life.

Q: **Can vibrational prayer be used for protection and clearing negative energy?**

A: Yes, vibrational prayer can be used for protection and clearing negative energy by focusing on visualising a protective shield, cultivating a positive mindset, and aligning your energy with the universe.

Q: **Can vibrational prayer be used in groups or communities?**

A: Yes, vibrational prayer can be used in groups or communities to amplify the energy and manifest collective desires.

Q: **Can vibrational prayer help me overcome addiction**

and negative patterns?

A: Yes, vibrational prayer can help you overcome addiction and negative patterns by focusing on visualising freedom and empowerment, cultivating a mindset of positivity and hope, and aligning your energy with the universe.

Q: **How can I use vibrational prayer to enhance my creativity and inspiration?**

A: To enhance your creativity and inspiration, focus on visualising new ideas and possibilities, cultivate a mindset of curiosity and openness, and align your energy with the universe.

Q: **Can vibrational prayer be used for protection and clearing of negative energy?**

A: Yes, vibrational prayer can be used for protection and clearing of negative energy by focusing on visualising a protective shield, cultivating a mindset of positivity and light, and aligning your energy with the universe.

Thank you for joining me on this journey of exploration and discovery. May the insights and wisdom shared in these pages continue to guide and inspire you on your own path. Remember, the power of prayer is always within you, waiting to be tapped. May you continue to vibrate at the highest frequency of love, light, and wisdom.

REFERENCE

[1] https://youtu.be/T6XOhZOOHek

[2] https://www.etymonline.com/word/prayer#:~:text=prayer%20(n.,of%20Latin%20adjective%20precaria%2 C%20fem.

[3] https://www.newworldencyclopedia.org/entry/Prayer#:~:text=The%20act%20of%20prayer%20is,practice%20in%20the%20modern%20world.

[4] https://www.marshmallowchallenge.com/blog/the-power-of-prayer-how-different-religions-and-beliefs-approach-prayer/

[5] https://www.britannica.com/topic/prayer/Forms-of-prayer-in-the-religions-of-the-world

[6] https://jesus.net/ways-of-prayer/

[7] https://en.wikipedia.org/wiki/Prayer#Act_of_prayer

[8] Want to unlock the full potential of the concepts of spirituality and religion explored in this book? Take the next step and dive into the comprehensive guide that will reveal all: https://www.godwinspiritnatureprophet.co.uk/shop/BEYOND-RELIGION-How-Spirituality-Can-Transform-Your-Life-

And-Heal-Your-World-PDF-COPY-p622698642

Spirit, Godwin (2024) *BEYOND RELIGION; How Spirituality can Transform Your Life And Heal Your World*

[9] https://www.josiedanielle.com/light-language#:~:text=It%20is%20a%20form%20of,language%20communicates%20to%20the%20soul.

[10] https://www.puregenerators.com/blog/what-is-light-language

[11] https://www.ncbi.nlm.nih.gov/pmc/articles/PMC5328245/

[12] https://selfmadeladies.com/power-gratitude-manifesting/

AUTHOR
Commander-In-Chief of Energy

Godwin Daramola, known to many as the Nature Prophet, is a visionary author, spiritual consultant, and inspirational speaker based in London, United Kingdom. With a profound connection to the natural world, spirituality and a deep understanding of the human experience, Godwin has dedicated his life to sharing wisdom, guidance, and spiritual insights with others.

As a sought-after consultant on spiritual matters, Godwin Daramola has worked with individuals and organisations from diverse backgrounds, offering his expertise and insights to facilitate personal growth, self-awareness, and spiritual evolution.

Godwin Daramola is a dynamic speaker and thought leader in spirituality and business. He has been featured in prominent publications, such as
 Forbes:
https://forbes.ge/en/how-spirit-nature-prophet-is-shifting-spiritual-consulting-wit h-accuracy-and-healing/

- Insider:
https://markets.financialcontent.com/streetinsider/news/article/marketersmedia-2 024-6-28-godwin-daramola-

introduces-new-method-combining-mental-techniques
-and-natural-energies

- NY Headlines:
https://nyheadline.com/press/godwin-daramola-introduces-new-method-combinin g-mental-techniques-and-natural-energies/114571

- Washington Headlines:
https://washingtonheadline.com/press/godwin-daramola-introduces-new-method- combining-mental-techniques-and-natural-energies/114571

- Think Business Today:
https://thinkbusinesstoday.com/news/godwin-daramola-introduces-new-method-c ombining-mental-techniques-and-natural-energies/479590

- Texas Today:
https://thetexastoday.com/press/godwin-daramola-introduces-new-method-combi ning-mental-techniques-and-natural-energies/114571

- Fox40:
http://www/wicz.com/Global/story.asp?S=50966981 and many others.

To stay updated on his latest works, events, and spiritual insights, follow him on social media or visit his website https://www.godwinspiritnatureprophet.co.uk/

He welcomes invitations to share his wisdom and perspectives at conferences, seminars, and other events that align with his areas of expertise.
If you're interested in inviting Godwin to speak at your event or need spiritual guidance, please contact him through his website or social media channels.

His social media handles are:
https://www.tiktok.com/@godwin_seer_psychic
https://facebook.com/ProphetGodwinSpirit
https://youtube.com/@godwinseerpsychic
https://www.instagram.com/godwin_seer_psychic
https://linktr.ee/GodwinSpiritNatureProphet

A Glimpse of Godwin Daramola

Commander-In-Chief of Energy Godwin Daramola, also known as Nature Prophet, is a renowned Business Management Consultant, Spiritist Center Founder, and Wellness Program Expert. With a career spanning over 20 years, Godwin Spirit has helped countless individuals and organizations achieve remarkable success. His profound understanding of human nature, combined with his gift of prophecy, allows him to guide and inspire others towards their desired goals. Godwin Daramola is dedicated to empowering individuals to unleash their full potential and live a purposeful life filled with abundance and harmony.

Godwin Daramola is an International Motivational Speaker, Lawyer and Business Consultant. He lives in England, United Kingdom.

Godwin Daramola is the Founder and CEO of Arte Business Advisers, a Frontier International Consulting Firm for Business Owners. He is also a Lawyer (LL.B and LL.M), and the Author of "SUCCESS AT THE DOOR" & "BEYOND RELIGION"

Scan the QR code to Contact Us